Adding & Subtracting Fractions BINGO!

Grades 4-6

Black & White Version

Postage Stamp	Double Postage Stamp	Triple Postage Stamp	Four Corners	Inside 4 Corners
Four Corners & Postage Stamp	Outside Diamond	Inside Diamond	Kite	Picnic Table
Inside Picture Frame	Outside Picture Frame	Plus Sign	Railroad Tracks	Clover Leaf
Full House	Mini Full House	Open House	Six pack	Nine Pack

7/24	9/12	1⅙	1	6/8
1/3	2/24	5/8	7/8	2/6
3/4	2/8	1⁹⁄₁₂	7/12	5/6
1/6	1⁷⁄₂₀	1¾	1⅐⁄₁₂	5/12
FREE	5/8	2/6	4/8	1/4

DEDICATION

This Book is dedicated to:

The Karner Blue Butterfly [1]in All Stages of Life,
And my Beautiful Maaa

Copyright

Blue Butterfly Books Math & Science Activities are Published by:

Blue Butterfly Books ™
Victoria BC
Canada V8S 4H9
www.ButterflyBooks.ca

ISBN-13: 978-0-9920530-6-2
ISBN-10: 0992053064

For other affordable, downloadable and printable Math and Science Games, feel free to visit:
www.math-lessons.ca
www.science-lessons.ca
Printed in the USA

Team Members for this Publication:
Editor: Sheila M. Hynes, *BA Hons, MES, York*
Contributor: Brian Stocker, *BA, MA, Santa Monica*
Contributor: D. A. Stocker, *BA, M Ed, Victoria*
Contributor: Dr. G.A. Stocker, *DDS, Toronto*

Table of Contents

Sustainability and Eco-Responsibility

Here at *Blue Butterfly Books*, trees are valuable to Mother Earth and the health and wellbeing of everyone. Minimizing our ecological footprint and effect on the environment, we choose *Create Space*, an eco-responsible printing company.

Electronic routing of our books reduces greenhouse gas emissions, worldwide. When a book order is received, the order is filled at the printing location closest to the client. Using environmentally friendly publishing technology, of the *Espresso* book printing machine, *Blue Butterfly Books* are printed as they are requested, saving thousands of books, and trees over time. This process offers the stable and viable alternative keeping healthy sustainability of our environment. All paper is acid-free, and interior paper stock is made from 30% post-consumer waste recycled material. Safe for children, *Create Space* also verifies the materials used in the print process are all CPSIA-compliant.

By purchasing this *Blue Butterfly Book*, you have supported Full Recovery and Preservation of The Karner Blue Butterfly. Our logo is the Karner Blue Butterfly, *Lycaeides melissa samuelis*, a rare and beautiful butterfly species whose only flower for propogation is the blue lupin flower. The Karner Butterfly is mostly found in the Great Lakes Region of the U.S.A. Recovery planning is in action, for the return of Karner Blue in Canada led by the National Recovery Strategy. The recovery goals and objectives are aimed at recreating suitable habitats for the butterfly and encourage the growth of blue lupines - the butterfly's natural ideal habitat.

For more info on the Karner Blue Butterfly feel free to visit:

http://www.albanypinebush.org/conservation/wildlife-management/karner-blue-butterfly-recovery

http://www.wiltonpreserve.org/conservation/karner-blue-butterfly.

http://www.natureconservancy.ca/en/what-we-do/resource-centre/featured-species/karner_blue.html.

This Book Supports Eco-Preservation of The Karner Blue Butterfly

Customization and White Label Service

Have your logo and school name on the front cover in a special edition produced for you're your school or institution; Visit: www.ButterflyBooks.ca

Or Feel Free to Contact us for details at:
info@ButterflyBooks.ca

Other Books, Study Guides, and Activities

Blue Butterfly Books™ also has:

Study Guides for High School and College Entrance in All Disciplines:
www.ButterflyBooks.ca, and;

Math and Science Activites
For our On-Line Downloadable Games and Free Lesson Plans:
www.math-lessons.ca
www.science-lessons.ca

Let's Begin!

Have Fun Learning Fractions with Bingo!

This Set of Math Cards is designed to achieve Learning Standard Requirements for Grade Levels 4-6 Mathematics and Communication. They are printed to be "Cut-Out" and made into a Bingo Game. This 27 Card Set includes 1 Caller's Sheet Card, 5 Winning Pattern Cards, 20 unique bingo cards and 1 foldable Tuck Box.

Fractions Bingo is a variation on the traditional BINGO game using fractions.

For the sake of simplicity, we have omitted the letters B I N G O at the top of the card, as this introduces another element which detracts from the purpose of the game – learning fractions.

For example, instead of calling out "Under the B," with the players making off the answer if it appears in the B column, the caller simply calls out the fraction equation, and the players can mark it off anywhere that it appears on the card.

This makes the game easier and faster.

Brain Developing:
- ✓ Spacial Functioning
- ✓ Memory
- ✓ Cognition
- ✓ Coordination

Mathematics Learning Objectives:
- ✓ Levels 4-6 Mathematics and Communication
- ✓ Fractions, Adding, Subtraction, Multiplication, Reasoning, memory, problem solving, and communication

Communication:
- ✓ Listening and observation skills and strategies to gain understanding
- ✓ Strategies for focusing attention and interpreting information
- ✓ Understanding, analyzing, synthesizing, or evaluating information
- ✓ Communication skills and strategies to interact/work effectively with others.
- ✓ Working collaboratively, solve problems, and perform tasks.

Summary

The basic play is that the *Caller*, calls out a fraction formula, for example, 2/6 + ¾, and the students have to then, perform the function and mark the answer ($1\frac{1}{12}$) on their BINGO cards until they have a winning pattern.

NOTE: the answers do NOT have to be in their lowest form. See below for a complete explanation.

BINGO Cards

20 unique bingo cards are included in the following pages, in addition to 1 Caller's Sheet, 5 Winning Pattern Cards, and 1 foldable Tuck Box. Ideally, each learner should receive a unique card, but if you have more than 20 learners in the class.

Alternatively, you can divide the class into smaller groups and have 2 or 3 groups playing at once.

The numbers on the cards are in different random colors. There is no pattern to the colors, and players cannot guess the answer by the pattern of coloring.

Decide the Winning Pattern

Before beginning of *the play*, first decide on the *winning pattern*. Traditionally, the winner has any 5 consecutive squares in a straight line, as is the same in tradituonal BINGO.

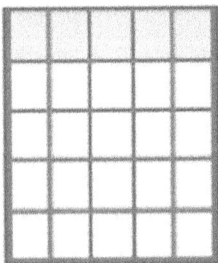

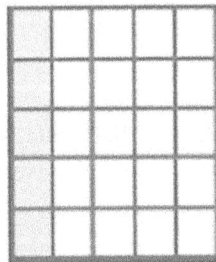

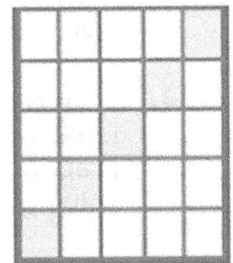

The straight line can be any 5 consecutive horizontal or vertical line, or a horizontal line from left to right or right to left.

See below for more advanced games and different patterns. Once learners become familiar with the game and the play, there is tremendous scope for variations and increasing the difficulty of the play.

The Play

The teacher, or a student, acts as the *Caller*, using the caller sheet below. The *Caller* calls out the numbers at random, and students place an 'X' in the square where the product of the call appears.

For example, in the Equivalent Fractions Bingo, if the Caller calls, 2/6 + 3/4, students place an 'X' over 11/12 that appears anywhere on their card.

It is very important for the Caller also mark off what they have called; otherwise, there is no way to confirm the winner.

The Caller continues to call out the fraction equation in a random fashion, marking off the *Call Sheet* as they go, with the students marking their BINGO cards appropriately.

The first person to fill the winning pattern on their BINGO card is the WINNER – at which time calls out to everyone, incuding, and especially, the Caller – "BINGO!"

The Caller must then check the person's card to confirm correct answers. If not correct, the play continues. If correct, a new Winning Pattern is decided by the Caller, and a new game begins. Providing Prizes for each Win is optional and can make it more fun.

Winning Patterns for Advanced Play
Letters

Letter C	Letter E	Letter F	Letter L	Letter N
Letter O	Letter T	Letter C	Letter U	Letter X

Objects

14

Postage Stamp	Double Postage Stamp	Triple Postage Stamp	Four Corners	Inside 4 Corners
Four Corners & Postage Stamp	Outside Diamond	Inside Diamond	Kite	Picnic Table
Inside Picture Frame	Outside Picture Frame	Plus Sign	Railroad Tracks	Clover Leaf
Full House	Mini Full House	Open House	Six pack	Nine Pack

FRACTIONS

1The word "fraction" is from the Latin *fractus*, meaning *broken*. A fraction is a number that represents part of a whole.

Common fractions are also called vulgars, meaning *commonplace*. They have a numerator and a denominator, the numerator representing a number of parts and the denominator telling how many of those parts make up a whole. An example is 3/4 in which the numerator, 3, tells us that the fraction represents 3 parts, and the denominator, 4, tells us that 4 parts, make up a whole.

The earliest fractions were reciprocals of integers, symbols representing one half, one third, one quarter, and so on. The numbers that we now call "decimals", were at one time, called "decimal fractions".

Geometry2

The translation of the ancient Greek word Geometry is: *"geo"*- "meaning earth", and *"metron"* - meaning "measurement"). It is a branch of mathematics entailing specifics of shape, size, relative position of figures, and the properties of space. A person who works in the field of geometry is called a *Mathematician*, though is also called a *Geometer*. Geometry concerns lengths, areas, and volumes, with elements in the West beginning around 6th Century BC. By the 3rd century, BC geometry was put into an "axiomatic" form by *Euclid*, a famous Mathematician and Geometer.

Later, the field of astronomy – making maps of the positions of the stars and planets, and describing the understanding between their movements, used the field of geometry extensivly for the following 1,500 years.

In *Euclid's* time there was no clear distinction between physical space and geometrical space. The visual nature of geometry makes it more accessible than other areas of mathematics – as well as spatially, brain developing, a more enjoyable and fun Art.

BINGO

2 *Bingo* is a game of chance played with randomly drawn numbers which players match against numbers that have been pre-printed on matrix cards. The game ends when the first person achieves a specified pattern from the drawn numbers. The winner is usually required to call out the word "Bingo!", which alerts the other players and caller of a possible win. All wins are checked for accuracy before the win is officially confirmed at which time the prize is secured and a new game is begun.

All Reference Material: *Wikipedia.com*. See EndNotes.

The Next pages include the 27 Cards.

Bingo Card Set Cut-Outs Begin Here on This Page

Winning Pattern Cards

Winning Pattern: Straight Line in Any Direction (Top 3 in 1 Cut-out for this card)
(For Caller to Choose from)

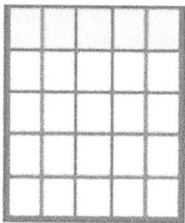

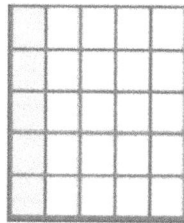

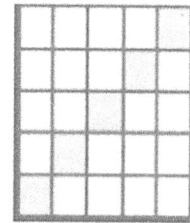

Winning Pattern: Letters (As 1 Cut-out)
(For Caller to Choose from)

Letter C	Letter E	Letter F	Letter L	Letter N
Letter O	Letter T	Letter C	Letter U	Letter X

Winning Pattern Objects
(For Caller to Choose from)

Postage Stamp	Double Postage Stamp	Triple Postage Stamp	Four Corners	Inside 4 Corners
Four Corners & Postage Stamp	Outside Diamond	Inside Diamond	Kite	Picnic Table
Inside Picture Frame	Outside Picture Frame	Plus Sign	Railroad Tracks	Clover Leaf
Full House	Mini Full House	Open House	Six pack	Nine Pack

Caller Sheet

1/2 + 1/4	2/3 + 1/4	1/2 + 4/8	3/8 + 1/4
2/3 + 1/6	1/4 + 5/8	2/3 – 1/4	6/8 – 1/2
1 ½ + 1/4	5/6 + 1/3	1/2 - 1/4	5/6 – 1/2
1/2 + 3/8	3/4 - 1/8	2/6 + 3/4	6/8 – 2/3
3/4 + 4/6	3/4 + 3/5	5/6 – 1/2	3/4 - 1/8
5/6 – 1/2	1/4 + 1/3	1/2 - 1/3	1/8 + 1/6

www.butterflybooks.ca

7/24	9/12	$1\frac{1}{6}$	1	6/8
1/3	2/24	5/8	7/8	2/6
3/4	2/8	$1\frac{5}{12}$	7/12	5/6
1/6	$1\frac{7}{20}$	$1\frac{3}{4}$	$1\frac{1}{12}$	5/12
FREE	5/8	2/6	4/8	1/4

4/8	5/12	9/12	5/8	7/24
$1\frac{1}{6}$	$1\frac{7}{20}$	7/8	2/6	7/12
FREE	2/6	1/4	3/4	1/6
$1\frac{3}{4}$	2/8	5/8	6/8	1
2/24	$1\frac{5}{12}$	1/3	5/6	$1\frac{1}{12}$

2/8	1	5/6	$1^5/_{12}$	5/8
7/8	FREE	1/6	$1^1/_{12}$	7/12
$1^7/_{20}$	6/8	9/12	1/4	4/8
7/24	$1^1/_6$	2/6	5/12	$1^3/_4$
1/3	5/8	3/4	2/6	2/24

$1^3/_4$	$1^1/_{12}$	1/6	$1^7/_{20}$	1/3
7/24	3/4	7/12	6/8	7/8
2/6	5/12	4/8	5/8	9/12
5/6	$1^5/_{12}$	2/24	FREE	2/6
$1^1/_6$	1/4	1	5/8	2/8

$1\frac{5}{12}$	1/6	2/6	4/8	5/8
FREE	6/8	1	5/12	2/8
5/6	7/24	7/12	3/4	7/8
2/6	$1\frac{1}{12}$	9/12	$1\frac{7}{20}$	1/4
5/8	$1\frac{3}{4}$	1/3	2/24	$1\frac{1}{6}$

www.butterflybooks.ca

5/6	$1\frac{3}{4}$	$1\frac{1}{12}$	5/12	$1\frac{5}{12}$
2/8	1/3	7/8	2/6	6/8
7/24	3/4	1/6	2/24	$1\frac{7}{20}$
FREE	4/8	2/6	1	1/4
$1\frac{1}{6}$	5/8	5/8	9/12	7/12

www.butterflybooks.ca

5/8	5/8	1/6	1/3	$1^{7}/_{20}$
$1^{3}/_{4}$	1/4	7/8	2/24	$1^{1}/_{12}$
$1^{5}/_{12}$	5/6	2/6	$1^{1}/_{6}$	5/12
6/8	1	7/24	7/12	3/4
4/8	9/12	2/6	2/8	FREE

www.butterflybooks.ca

2/8	$1^{5}/_{12}$	4/8	7/24	5/6
5/8	2/6	$1^{7}/_{20}$	5/12	5/8
$1^{1}/_{6}$	7/8	2/24	2/6	6/8
FREE	$1^{1}/_{12}$	1	$1^{3}/_{4}$	7/12
9/12	1/3	3/4	1/6	1/4

www.butterflybooks.ca

3/4	5/12	1/6	$1\frac{1}{12}$	$1\frac{5}{12}$
FREE	7/24	5/8	1/3	4/8
$1\frac{1}{6}$	7/12	$1\frac{7}{20}$	2/6	$1\frac{3}{4}$
9/12	2/6	2/8	7/8	5/6
1	2/24	1/4	5/8	6/8

www.butterflybooks.ca

2/8	$1\frac{3}{4}$	1/3	3/4	7/8
6/8	1/6	2/6	$1\frac{1}{6}$	4/8
2/6	FREE	$1\frac{5}{12}$	1/4	5/12
$1\frac{7}{20}$	2/24	5/8	9/12	7/24
7/12	$1\frac{1}{12}$	5/6	5/8	1

www.butterflybooks.ca

1/3	2/24	$1\frac{1}{6}$	2/6	5/8
5/12	$1\frac{7}{20}$	5/6	**5/8**	$1\frac{5}{12}$
1/6	3/4	6/8	1	**9/12**
FREE	**7/8**	7/12	$1\frac{3}{4}$	2/6
4/8	$1\frac{1}{12}$	**1/4**	2/8	**7/24**

www.butterflybooks.ca

1/3	6/8	$1\frac{1}{6}$	$1\frac{5}{12}$	1
7/12	3/4	2/24	2/6	**1/4**
5/8	2/8	5/12	4/8	$1\frac{3}{4}$
9/12	**FREE**	**1/6**	2/6	5/6
7/24	5/8	7/8	$1\frac{7}{20}$	$1\frac{1}{12}$

www.butterflybooks.ca

5/6	$1\frac{7}{20}$	2/8	FREE	$1\frac{1}{8}$
7/8	9/12	4/8	$1\frac{1}{12}$	2/6
1/4	2/24	1/6	3/4	1
6/8	$1\frac{3}{4}$	7/12	5/8	5/8
5/12	2/6	7/24	$1\frac{5}{12}$	1/3

www.butterflybooks.ca

7/24	$1\frac{1}{8}$	$1\frac{1}{12}$	5/12	5/6
2/24	2/6	4/8	FREE	1/6
3/4	$1\frac{3}{4}$	$1\frac{5}{12}$	7/12	2/8
1	7/8	9/12	5/8	6/8
$1\frac{7}{20}$	5/8	2/6	1/4	1/3

www.butterflybooks.ca

1/6	5/8	$1\frac{5}{12}$	2/6	9/12
5/6	2/8	5/8	2/24	7/8
4/8	5/12	3/4	1/3	$1\frac{1}{6}$
7/12	$1\frac{3}{4}$	$1\frac{7}{20}$	$1\frac{1}{12}$	7/24
6/8	1	FREE	1/4	2/6

www.butterflybooks.ca

7/12	7/24	3/4	5/12	6/8
5/8	$1\frac{1}{12}$	2/24	1/4	5/8
4/8	$1\frac{7}{20}$	$1\frac{3}{4}$	2/8	FREE
2/6	2/6	5/6	1/6	$1\frac{1}{6}$
7/8	$1\frac{5}{12}$	9/12	1	1/3

www.butterflybooks.ca

1/6	5/8	2/6	$1\frac{1}{12}$	3/4
2/6	5/12	$1\frac{7}{20}$	1/4	2/8
5/8	7/8	5/6	7/24	1/3
4/8	$1\frac{1}{6}$	$1\frac{5}{12}$	2/24	6/8
9/12	1	7/12	FREE	$1\frac{3}{4}$

www.butterflybooks.ca

7/24	3/4	$1\frac{5}{12}$	1	5/6
5/12	4/8	1/4	2/24	1/3
$1\frac{1}{6}$	1/6	5/8	2/8	$1\frac{1}{12}$
$1\frac{7}{20}$	5/8	6/8	9/12	2/6
2/6	FREE	$1\frac{3}{4}$	7/8	7/12

www.butterflybooks.ca

2/8	1	1/6	5/12	5/6
1/4	$1\frac{1}{6}$	9/12	2/24	2/6
7/12	$1\frac{7}{20}$	$1\frac{1}{12}$	5/8	7/8
1/3	FREE	$1\frac{3}{4}$	3/4	5/8
7/24	2/6	4/8	6/8	$1\frac{5}{12}$

www.butterflybooks.ca

$1\frac{5}{12}$	2/6	$1\frac{1}{12}$	7/8	5/8
1/3	FREE	1/4	4/8	5/6
2/8	1	3/4	1/6	7/12
$1\frac{7}{20}$	$1\frac{3}{4}$	9/12	$1\frac{1}{6}$	2/24
7/24	6/8	5/8	5/12	2/6

www.butterflybooks.ca

Tuck Box for Storage of your Bingo Cards

- With scissors, cut around outside of Tuck Box Frame from next 2 pages, first page being
- the left side of your tuckbox, and 2nd page being the right side – and Glue the two together
- Line-up and Glue left side to right side
- Make folds along all inner lines
- Glue far-left side edge < to > far-right side edge (1 cm each side)
- Glue bottom-left side upward (1 cm)

Fractions BINGO!

Blue Butterfly Books™

www.ButterflyBooks.ca

CONGRATULATIONS!

You made it!! You have made yourself a Set of *Bingo!* Cards that can improve your Learning Fractions in Math for Hours and Hours of Fun. Thank you for playing with

Blue Butterfly Books ™   in our mandate to make Learning Math easy and fun!

ENDNOTES:

1. Fractions. In *Wikipedia*. http: //en. wiki/fractions

2. Bingo. In *Wikipedia*. http: //en. wiki/bingo

3. Blue Butterfly. In *Microsoft Clipart*. Retrieved October 15, 2013 from: http://office.microsoft.com/en-CA/images/results.aspx?qu=blue%20butterfly&ex=2#ai:MP900314069|

NOTES